THE STORY OF THE MEMPHIS GRIZZLIES

Tyus Jones

Desmond Bane

A HISTORY OF HOOPS
THE STORY OF THE
MEMPHIS
GRIZZLIES

JIM WHITING

Mike Conley

CREATIVE EDUCATION / CREATIVE PAPERBACKS

Published by Creative Education and Creative Paperbacks
P.O. Box 227, Mankato, Minnesota 56002
Creative Education and Creative Paperbacks are imprints of
The Creative Company
www.thecreativecompany.us

Design and production by Blue Design (www.bluedes.com)
Art direction by Rita Marshall
Production layout by Rachel Klimpel and Ciara Beitlich

Photographs by Alamy (Reuters), AP Images (Carlos Avila Gonzalez, David J.
Phillip, Mark J. Terrill, Steve Yeater), Corbis (Tim Sharp), Getty (Bill Baptist,
David Berding, Andrew D. Bernstein/NBAE, Kevin C. Cox, Jonathan Daniel,
Focus On Sport, Justin Ford, Thearon W. Henderson, Jason Miller, Layne
Murdoch, Joe Murphy, Greg Nelson, Christian Petersen, Ezra Shaw, Jamie
Squire), Newscom (Mark Halmas/Icon SMI), Shutterstock (Brocreative)

Library of Congress Cataloging-in-Publication Data
Names: Whiting, Jim, 1943- author.
Title: The story of the Memphis Grizzlies / by Jim Whiting.
Description: Mankato, Minnesota : Creative Education/Creative
    Paperbacks, 2023. | Series: Creative Sports. A History of Hoops | Includes
    index. | Audience: Ages 8-12 | Audience: Grades 4-6 | Summary: "Middle
    grade basketball fans are introduced to the extraordinary history of
    NBA's Memphis Grizzlies with a photo-laden narrative of their greatest
    successes and losses"-- Provided by publisher.
Identifiers: LCCN 2022009510 (print) | LCCN 2022009511 (ebook) | ISBN
    9781640266315 (library binding) | ISBN 9781682771877 (paperback) | ISBN
    9781640007727 (ebook)
Subjects: LCSH: Memphis Grizzlies (Basketball team)--History--Juvenile
    literature.
Classification: LCC GV885.52.M46 W553 2023 (print) | LCC GV885.52.M46
    (ebook) | DDC 796.323/640976819--dc23/eng/20220224
LC record available at https://lccn.loc.gov/2022009510
LC ebook record available at https://lccn.loc.gov/2022009511

Rudy Gay

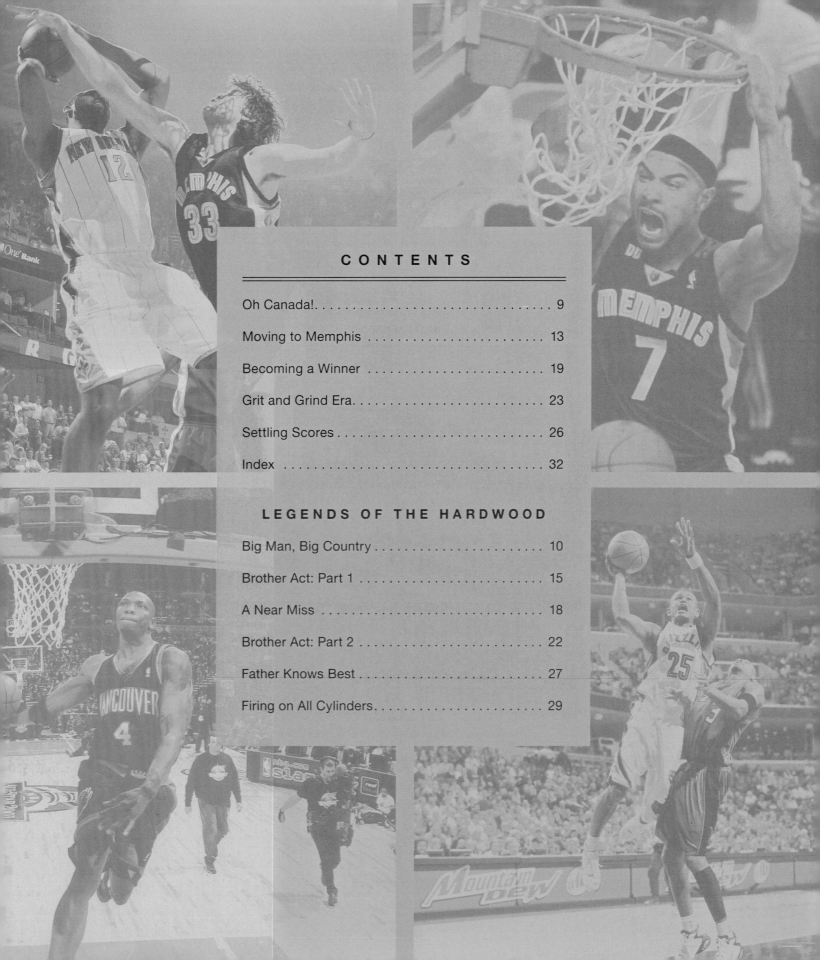

CONTENTS

LEGENDS OF THE HARDWOOD

Ja Morant

OH CANADA!

Early in a game on January 9, 2022, Los Angeles Lakers' guard Avery Bradley stole the ball from Memphis Grizzlies' point guard Ja Morant and raced toward the hoop. Morant trailed Bradley by more than 10 feet. As Bradley left his feet for what appeared to be an easy lay-in, Morant suddenly flashed into the picture. With both hands nearly three feet above the rim, he blocked the shot. He jumped so high that his head grazed the backboard. After blocking the shot, Morant controlled the loose ball and sped downcourt.

Many basketball authorities compared Morant's play to LeBron James's epic block in the 2016 National Basketball Association (NBA) Finals that helped the Cleveland Cavaliers take the title. The comparison was high praise and one of the key highlights in Grizzlies history.

That history began back in 1995, when the NBA expanded into Canada. The league granted franchises to Toronto in Ontario and Vancouver in British Columbia. The Vancouver owners wanted to name their team the Mounties, after the famous Royal Canadian Mounted Police (RCMP). The RCMP didn't want a team named after them. Fans didn't, either.

LEGENDS
OF THE HARDWOOD

BRYANT REEVES
CENTER
HEIGHT: 7-FOOT-0
GRIZZLIES SEASONS: 1995–2001

BIG MAN, BIG COUNTRY

Bryant Reeves hailed from Gans, a small town in rural Oklahoma. "He talked more passionately about farming and farm animals than he did basketball," laughed Grizzlies teammate Blue Edwards. Reeves was nicknamed "Big Country" while playing with the Oklahoma State University basketball team. He led his college team to the 1995 NCAA Final Four and became the Grizzlies' first-ever draft pick. His large size made him a natural fit for a team named after a large bear. Reeves reached his peak in his third season with 16.3 points and 7.9 rebounds per game. Then he had health issues. The team kept losing. Fans booed him. "He gave it his all. As a player, that's all you can do," said Hall of Fame center Patrick Ewing. In 2018, a documentary film called *Finding Big Country* featured Reeves.

After a naming contest, the team became the Grizzlies. Those ferocious bears roam the rugged backcountry of British Columbia. Unfortunately, the team wasn't very ferocious even though it featured massive rookie center, Bryant "Big Country" Reeves. The Grizzlies won their first two games in the 1995–96 season. Then they lost the next 19. Later that season, they lost 23 in a row. It was a record for the longest one-season losing streak in the NBA. They finished the season with a league-worst 15–67 record.

In the 1996 NBA Draft, Vancouver took power forward Shareef Abdur-Rahim as the third overall pick. He was an immediate sensation. He led the team in scoring with nearly 19 points a game. He finished third in balloting for NBA Rookie of the Year. Unfortunately, the Grizzlies continued to struggle. They finished 14–68. Once again, they were at the bottom of the league. "The losing has been tough," Abdur-Rahim said. "The only thing I can control is my effort and my attitude going forward... You do your best, keep on fighting, and keep on battling." Vancouver improved to 19 wins the following season and avoided having the league's worst record. Disputes between league owners and players delayed the start of the 1998–99 season. Vancouver dropped to 8–42. The team's winning percentage of .160 was the seventh worst in NBA history. Rookie point guard Mike Bibby, the second overall pick in the 1998 NBA Draft, offered some excitement. He averaged 13 points and 6.5 assists a game.

MOVING TO MEMPHIS

The Grizzlies had the second overall draft pick again in 1999. They chose high-flying guard Steve Francis. Some people thought he might be the next Michael Jordan. Francis refused to play for Vancouver, though. He wanted a team that could give him more media exposure, and Vancouver was too remote. The Grizzlies made a three-way trade involving Francis. They netted four players and several draft picks, but it wasn't much help. The team won just 22 games in 1999–2000. The following season, they won five games in a row. They had never done that before. But they ended 23–59. They traded Bibby and Abdur-Rahim.

Basketball in Vancouver was doomed. The constant losing kept fans away. The Grizzlies decided to move. They considered eight cities and chose Memphis, Tennessee. It was the city's first major professional sports franchise. The Federal Express (FedEx) package delivery company is headquartered in Memphis. The company paid $100 million for the right to name the team's new home arena FedExForum. The company also wanted to change the name from Grizzlies to Express. The NBA rejected that change. "As a matter of long-standing policy, we don't permit teams to be named after commercial entities," said NBA official Mike Bass. So even though the only big bears in the area were in zoos, the team remained the Grizzlies.

Shareef Abdur-Rahim

The team didn't have better luck in its new home. It won only 23 games. However, rookie Spanish-born power forward/center Pau Gasol, who was part of the Abdur-Rahim trade, was an immediate sensation. He averaged almost 18 points and 9 rebounds per game. He was the only Grizzlies player to play in all 82 of the team's games that season. He won the NBA Rookie of the Year Award. His selection didn't surprise Sacramento Kings head coach Rick Adelman. "There isn't anyone close," Adelman said. "Night after night he just keeps putting up the numbers. He is really a solid player."

But Memphis overall wasn't much better in 2002–03. Its record was 28–54. Still, it was the best so far in the team's history. Memphis fans saw reason for optimism. The Grizzlies had acquired point guard Jason Williams as part of the Bibby trade. He led the team in assists that year. A mid-season trade added long-range small forward/shooting guard Mike Miller.

Jason Williams

PAU GASOL
POWER FORWARD/CENTER
HEIGHT: 7-FOOT-0
GRIZZLIES SEASONS: 2001–08

BROTHER ACT: PART 1

Pau Gasol began playing basketball in his native country, Spain, when he was seven. He soon fell in love with the NBA. "My grandfather used to buy me an NBA magazine every month," he said. "I collected the posters that came in the magazine and put them in my room." Years later, former American standout Walt Szczerbiak, who played in Spain during the 1970s, watched him play. "He was a matchup nightmare for anyone who played against him," Szczerbiak said. In 2001, Gasol became the third overall selection in the NBA Draft. "It's the best day of my life," he said. Gasol averaged nearly 19 points and 9 rebounds a game throughout his 7 seasons in Memphis.

Dillon Brooks

LEGENDS
OF THE HARDWOOD

Jerry West

A NEAR MISS

The biggest name in the 2003 NBA Draft was high school superstar LeBron
James. Memphis had one of the worst records in the league the previous
season. The Grizzlies became part of the draft lottery. If they won, they would
draft James. The lottery came down to three teams: Cleveland Cavaliers, Denver
Nuggets, and Memphis Grizzlies. Each team had its name in a sealed envelope.
NBA deputy commissioner Russ Granik opened the first one. It said Denver,
which meant the Nuggets were out. If the next envelope said Cleveland, the
Grizzlies would get James. But Granik drew Memphis instead. Cleveland won and
took the upcoming superstar. "It was devastating to the franchise to not have
that pick," said general manager Jerry West.

BECOMING A WINNER

The 2003–04 season was a completely different story from what had come before. The Grizzlies notched 50 wins and qualified for the playoffs for the first time. Few NBA teams had ever gone from 50 or more losses one season to 50 or more wins the next. A major factor was coach Hubie Brown. He was named NBA Coach of the Year. "In my mind, there is no way that we could have accomplished a 50-win season without him coaching this team," said general manager Jerry West. Another factor was the team's never-give-up attitude. Memphis had 14 fourth-quarter comeback wins. It was an NBA season best.

This newfound success was a team effort. Eight players averaged 20 minutes or more of playing time per game. "It's a great turnaround for the franchise," Gasol said. "We've surprised ourselves. I can't believe where we are." The Grizzlies faced defending NBA champion San Antonio Spurs in the first round of the 2003–04 playoffs. The Spurs swept the series.

Memphis maintained the momentum in 2004–05 with 45 wins and qualified for the playoffs again. They faced the top-seeded Phoenix Suns in the first round. Again, they were swept. "It's hard right now," Gasol said. "Maybe after watching and seeing yourself [in a replay of the game] you can learn." The Grizzlies learned from their mistakes and won 13 of their first 18 games the following season. They finished with 49 wins. Gasol became the team's first All-Star. Memphis faced the Dallas Mavericks in the first round of the playoffs, but lost again.

Memphis fans looked forward to another successful season in 2006–07. They were excited by rookie small forward Rudy Gay. "We acquired one of the very best prospects from this year's draft," said West. "Even though he is a very young player at 19, the talent of this young man is phenomenal, and we are hopeful people will enjoy watching this kind of athlete." People did enjoy watching him. Fans chanted, "Rudy! Rudy! Rudy!" whenever he had the ball. He was named to the NBA All-Rookie First Team. Unfortunately, Gasol had broken his foot before the season started. He missed the first 22 games. The Grizzlies never recovered. They plunged to 22–60.

The Grizzlies couldn't gain any traction in the 2007–08 season. Wins were few and far between. In February, Memphis traded Gasol to the Lakers. Many people criticized the move. New general manager Chris Wallace thought the team was losing so much, it needed to make some bold changes to get back to winning. "We're a 13-win team," Wallace said, "so when you're in that situation, you've got to make moves." Memphis received four players and two future draft choices. One of the players was center Marc Gasol, Pau Gasol's younger brother. It is the only time in NBA history that one brother was traded for another. Marc joined the Grizzlies for the 2008–09 season. He averaged 12 points a game. He was named to the NBA All-Rookie Second Team. Still, the Grizzlies won just 24 games. They were one of the NBA's youngest teams. The average age of the starters was just 21.

One young player was point guard Mike Conley, who was just 19 when the Grizzlies chose him fourth overall in the 2007 NBA Draft. Another was shooting guard O.J. Mayo, age 20, who was part of an eight-player trade that brought him to Memphis. He led all rookies in the 2008–09 season with an average of 18.5 points per game. He finished second in voting for NBA Rookie of the Year.

Rudy Gay

MARC GASOL
CENTER
HEIGHT: 7-FOOT-1
GRIZZLIES SEASONS: 2008–2019

BROTHER ACT: PART 2

Marc Gasol's nickname in high school was the "Big Burrito." "Lose weight," a coach told him. He did. Gasol played for the Spanish national team that won the 2006 World Championships. "I saw that I could [go] against the best players in the world," he said. He barely missed playing for the Grizzlies at the same time as his brother. In February 2008, the Grizzlies traded Pau to the Lakers. Part of the package included Los Angeles giving Memphis the draft rights to Marc. He was playing in Europe at the time. He signed with the Grizzlies several months later. By the end of his Memphis career, he was just 50 points shy of being the team's all-time scoring leader. Pau ranks fourth.

The team also benefited from coach Marc Iavaroni's team-first attitude. "Guys are really buying into what Coach has been telling us," Conley said. "And after you see that team basketball gets you wins, guys make it a point to work on it."

Despite that team-first attitude, the Grizzlies saw little improvement. The Grizzlies traded for power forward Zach Randolph before the 2009–10 season. The Grizzlies started off at 1–8. By the end of January, they had rebounded to 25–21. "Zach has been the catalyst behind our turnaround," Wallace said. "Other teams have to double-team him, so there's more room out there for O. J. Mayo and Rudy Gay to operate." The Grizzlies couldn't maintain that pace, though. They finished 40–42. They missed the playoffs for the fourth season in a row. Even so, the increasing talent in Memphis had fans hopeful.

GRIT AND GRIND ERA

The Grizzlies acquired the nickname "grit and grind" for their style of playing. They led the league in steals in 2010–11. Nonetheless, hardly anyone gave Memphis a chance against the Spurs in the opening round of the playoffs. The mighty Spurs won 61 games that season. It was the best record in the NBA's Western Conference. Memphis, on the other hand, had just 46 wins. In addition, Gay had suffered a season-ending injury two months earlier.

The Grizzlies beat the Spurs in San Antonio, 101–98, in the first game when small forward Shane Battier sank a three-pointer in the final moments. San Antonio took the next game. Memphis took advantage of their home court and won the following two. The Spurs won Game 5 in overtime. A sellout crowd packed FedExForum for Game 6. The Grizzlies roared to a 27–16 first-quarter lead. With less than five minutes left, the Spurs surged ahead. Randolph took over the game. He scored 13 points. The Grizzlies pulled away for a 99–91 win. It was the first time that the Grizzlies had won a playoff series! "Not a lot of people knew about us coming in, but we certainly have made some noise and turned some heads," said coach Lionel Hollins. One turned head belonged to Spurs forward Tim Duncan. "We were hoping at some point that they would fold under the pressure, make some mistakes … and they didn't," he said.

Memphis pushed Oklahoma City to the limit in the next round. But Memphis lost, 4 games to 3. The Grizzlies went 41–25 in the lockout-shortened 2011–12 season. They faced the Los Angeles Clippers in the first round of the playoffs. The Clippers won the seven-game series. Two Memphis losses were by a single point. A third defeat came in overtime.

The Grizzlies opened the 2012–13 season 12–2. They never looked back. They raced to a franchise-best 56 wins. Marc Gasol set the tone for "grit and grind." He was named the league's Defensive Player of the Year. "It's a great award to receive," said his brother Pau. "Great recognition, a great accomplishment for him, and I'm just very proud of what he's been able to do and who he has become as a player and as a person. So, I'm a proud big brother."

Zach Randolph

SETTLING SCORES

emphis settled some scores in the playoffs in 2012–2013. It beat the Clippers in the first round, 4 games to 2. Then it knocked off Oklahoma City in the next round. The Grizzlies advanced to the Western Conference finals for the first time. "It's hard to put into words how important this is to the franchise," said general manager Chris Wallace. "It was just a few years ago we got our first playoff win." But San Antonio had too much firepower. The Spurs swept the series.

The team won 50 games in 2013–14. They faced the Thunder in the first round of the playoffs. In a tight series, the Grizzlies won three of the first five games. All were in overtime. But Oklahoma City won the next two games and took the series. Shooting guard Courtney Lee and small forward Jeff Green helped the Grizzlies to 55 wins the next year. Memphis brushed aside the Portland Trail Blazers in the first round of the playoffs, 4 games to 1. Then the team met the Golden State Warriors in the next round. The Warriors' 67–15 record was sixth-best in NBA history. The Grizzlies won two of the first three games. But Golden State easily won the next three to defeat Memphis.

The Grizzlies clawed their way back to the playoffs in 2015–16. But the Spurs kicked them out in the first round. Nearly the same thing happened the following season. Three losing seasons followed, though Ja Morant was named NBA Rookie of the Year in 2019–20. He helped the Grizzlies to return to the playoffs in 2020–21. So did rookie small forward/shooting guard Desmond Bane. Memphis lost in the first round to the Jazz.

JA MORANT
POINT GUARD
HEIGHT: 6-FOOT-3
GRIZZLIES SEASONS:
2019–PRESENT

FATHER KNOWS BEST

Even though Ja Morant was his South Carolina high school's all-time leading scorer, national recruiting services didn't rank him. By accident, a coach at Murray State University in Kentucky saw Morant play in a pickup game. He was impressed enough to offer him a scholarship. Morant's father said, "Every parent wants their child to play at a big-time program, but what I realized is, don't go where you want to be, go to where they want you." Morant took his father's advice. He became the first NCAA player to average at least 20 points and 10 assists per game in a single season. The Grizzlies made him the second overall selection in the 2019 NBA Draft.

MEMPHIS GRIZZLIES

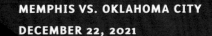

LEGENDS
OF THE HARDWOOD

FIRING ON ALL CYLINDERS

Driven by hot shooting and controlling the backboards, the Grizzlies jumped out to a 72–36 halftime lead. They did even better in the second half, adding another 80 points to win 152–79. The 73-point difference is the largest in NBA history. Incredibly, Memphis did it without their sparkplug, Ja Morant. In his absence, power forward Jaren Jackson Jr. led the team with 27 points. Eight other players scored in double figures. "It feels great to be in the history books, especially in front of our home crowd," said point/shooting guard De'Anthony Melton, who scored 19 points. "Everybody contributed, everybody played hard, and we all got to get in the game."

MEMPHIS GRIZZLIES

The two young players came into their own the following season as Memphis matched the previous year's win total of 38 by late January/early February. The Grizzlies went on to tie their franchise-best 56 wins. Morant averaged more than 27 points and 7 assists per game. He was named the league's Most Improved Player. Bane averaged more than 18 points per game. So did small forward/shooting guard Dillon Brooks.

Memphis faced the Minnesota Timberwolves in the first round of the playoffs. Minnesota won the first game. The Grizzlies came back to win Game 2. In three of the following four games, Memphis trailed by double digits in the fourth quarter. They came back each time to win and take the series, 4 games to 2.

The Grizzlies took on Golden State in the conference semifinals. The teams split the first two games. Morant suffered a knee injury late in Game 3. He didn't play the rest of the series. The Warriors won in six games. Despite the defeat, Brooks remained upbeat. "We're young and they're getting old," he said. "They know that we are going to come every single year."

The Grizzlies have come a long way since their start in Canada. They have assembled a solid lineup of young players who know their roles. They are committed to playing tough defense. Fans hope to soon see a championship banner fly in FedExForum.

Jaren Jackson Jr.

INDEX

Tony Allen